The Language of Good Table Manners

The Language of Good Table Manners

Stimulating a World of Career Advancement and Leadership Skills

Kelly McBride Loft

The cover design features a distinctly designed spoon image. It is a mote spoon from the 1700's which was utilized prior to the American Revolution. It served as a scoop to remove loose tea leaves from teacups. Our tools are crafted to assist with functionality. Our dining tables, despite hundreds of years of changes, remain steadfastly consistent in order to continually assist with our personal functionality.

The Language of Good Table Manners
Stimulating a World of Career Advancement and Leadership Skills
Is part of the Plan Like A Chef™ Event *Master* Series of Books

This book is dedicated to the inspiration in creativity because without art, music, literature, poetry, dance and the culinary arts, we, by nature, would be inclined to focus on the fear of failure.

Table of Contents

The Language of Good Table Manners

SKILLFULNESS IS DRIVEN by a devotion to one's craft. It used to be that a path to success could be obtained by being gifted with two skills: one aesthetic and one intellectual. Times have changed. There is a need to be gifted with at least three life skills. Why? Careers in one field tend to last for less than one decade. Reinventing oneself isn't impossible for career transitions; there just needs to be at least one reliable communication skill, in addition to philosophical and cognitive skills. Some call a reliable constant in their life to be their *true north*, as a compass guide for direction in life. This significant lifestyle guide is the language of good table manners. It is at this special place that we learn how to treat others well, how to conduct ourselves in public, and how to respond within the structure of our families. Our dining tables are our *true north*.

The Logic and Importance of Dining

THE EDUCATIONAL PROCESS begins when we acknowledge the logic and the importance of dining. We come to our tables for nourishment, for conversation, and for bonding. It is from this beautiful focal point that we begin our passage to master multi-tasking. How we talk to others and how we develop our first interactive voice happens during these quintessential dining experiences. It is a legacy lifestyle, for complete life skills, that provides the tools for an individual's progress and success.

It is from the teachable table that we reinforce the stability of style. From daily dining to life celebrations, the focus is around food service and relationship development. This is the basis and the continuity for the language of good table manners.

The need to dine seems so obvious; yet, "selfie" encouragement seems to slow the prioritizing of the art of conversational table communication. There is only so much contemplation time in a day. If that precious thought time is comprised of interacting, eating, working, learning, and electronic absorption, then some thought time should be reserved to think of others with the basic three R's: respect, responding, and reflection.

The Power of Respect

AN EMOTIONALLY EVOLVED civilization encourages respect for food. The first dining "etiquette" rules were not established by royalty; rather, the laws of food safety and hygiene have existed since biblical times. Written respect for one's food dates back to the 1st century BCE with the dietary guidelines of kashrut and halāl. Simply put, if the "rules" for food preparation were not followed, one could die of diseases. Prayers of respect for nourishment were enacted along with the "laws" for food preparation. These acts of reverence are still followed by millions of people today. Traditionally and still today, it is an honor to break bread. This has been integrated into the concept of good manners. It is proper to break bread with one's hands and pass the bread around the table. The acclaimed French *boulangeries* have taught the world the art of baking bread and this special dining occurrence should be enjoyed frequently or at least once per week, if possible. Sharing a loaf of bread reinforces the essence of dining sensibility. The tradition has lasted for over 2,000 years for good reasons.

The Price Painfully Paid

THERE IS A saying that we are what we eat. Actually, a more modern version is that we are how we eat. Currently, we are at a crucial turning point – a precipice. Either we can choose to keep our dining values safe and move forward or we can choose to relinquish our socialization skills and move backwards. Preservation of a quality dining lifestyle begins with the knowledge that significant political conflicts were fought for food and spices. These are just a few:

From 1602 – 1663 the Dutch-Portuguese War was fought over the spice trade for pepper, cloves, and nutmeg.

In February of 1623, the Amboyna Massacre occurred in the Spice Islands, now known as Indonesia. Twenty men were tortured and executed, by agents of the Dutch East India Trading Company.

From the mid-1600s to 1807 forced labor, torture, and abhorrent abuse supported the Caribbean sugar plantations.

From 1680 to 1800, the Dutch East India Trading Company demanded forced labor, penalties, torture, and the deportation of the native people in the Spice Islands.

The American Revolution was initiated from the high taxation on goods and tea. The Boston Tea Party occurred on December 16, 1773, a day in which high valued tea was tossed into the Boston Harbor. This incited over eight years of war between the heavily taxed colonists and the British.

There were the patriots of the French Revolution who initiated a war over food shortages and a lack of a quality lifestyle from 1789 to 1799.

Mahatma Gandhi led The Salt March Period during the spring of 1930.

Forced labor, cruelty, murder, treachery, manipulation, and greed encompass the history of many food items that are purchased for very small amounts of money in the modern era. Abundance has created a genre of ungratefulness. It is a paradox, that during today's era of obtainable sustenance, we are lackadaisical about being appreciative of an advanced lifestyle that evolved from oppression, armed conflicts, intense battles, and loss of life. Today, we have created a war against ourselves – a war against our own place at the dining table.

The Civility of Beverages

IN THE MID-1600s, over two thousand coffee houses offered hot beverages in London. By the mid-1700s, tea was being sold in the London coffee houses. It was enormously popular. (This was prior to The American Revolution and The French Revolution.) Coffee and tea consumption still encourage lingering conversation.

Between the late 1700s through the 1800s, particularly in Russia, samovars were widely used. A samovar is a brass or ceramic heating vessel that ranges from two feet to four feet tall. This was traditionally placed in the center of the dining table. Ornate and functional, the heating vessel, fueled by coal, would heat a kettle of water positioned at the top, for tea. It also simultaneously heated water in the middle section of the samovar vessel, keeping the family warm during dining on long, cold nights. This enhanced the family's table gathering. Consider this. During the time period of the late 1700s through the mid-1800s, there was a resurgence of creativity with master artists, writers, poets, and musicians, which is also known as the age of Romanticism. Was this a cathartic coincidence? There were no television sets or electronic distractions, which left more time for creativity and conversation. This quality dining time would have enhanced musical talent, literature development, and scholastic fortitude. No longer do we linger at our dining or kitchen tables. Have we traded the zeal generated from our table stimulus for a quick meal, domesticated convenience, and predictable plastic utensils? We are being short-changed by a lack of emphasis on essential dining and inspirational conversation. To-go swag bag dining and loud music, in which patrons need to yell across the table, disrupt calm dining. Awareness creates a desire to improve; but, first, there has to be a willingness to improve. It is not a simple solution to only understand the past; it is a simple solution to understand the priorities for civility. This trickles down to how we talk to each other, how we react to each other, and how we become a developed society.

The Interrupted Meal

THE INTERRUPTED MEAL has been given much thought for centuries. Several of the Dutch master paintings of Willem Kalf in the 1600s depicted the interrupted meal through still life art featuring half-eaten fruit and half-filled glasses of wine. Another Dutch master painter, Balthasar van der Ast, in the 1600s, featured vibrant cut flowers with insects. Set against black backgrounds, the chiaroscuro impacts of an artisan's skill make the paintings very appealing. Some consider that the beautiful table settings conceal the symbolic messages that the paintings represent interrupted meals from the deaths of loved ones. Today, we think nothing of having our own meals constantly interrupted by electronic transmissions, tardiness, and a lack of organization. When interruptions are allowed and even enabled by the host or hostess, the pattern of poor manners is perpetuated. Disruptive distractions need to be eliminated in order to allow our emotionally evolved minds synchronicity with thousands of years of culinary and social development. This isn't about an inability to accept change; rather, it is the silent force generated from hand held devices and a lack of concern that is restraining human interaction from our sacred, trusted tables.

Accelerated lifestyles can compromise the character of our kitchens, the character of our dining table moments, and the character of our family moments. A fast food lifestyle diminishes the home-cooked aromas from our kitchens. Not being able to respond to the aromas of home-cooked meals robs us of the experiences to exercise one of our great senses – the sense of smell. The deprivation, from stimulating aromas during our dining moments, denies necessary cognitive responsiveness for ingesting precious sustenance, creating good memories, and enjoying camaraderie. Without table stimulus we lessen and suppress the responsiveness in areas of our brain usage, which is a great emotional loss.

In less than a half of a century, our food preparation time has gone from hours to a personal choice of five to ten minutes. Because of time constraints and an abundance of processed foods, meal preparation is minimalized. Additionally, this expediting of the food preparation time has accelerated the eating experience. A meal can be eaten in a few short minutes. Now, add the electronic device connectedness. The result has lessened the quality dining experience, which reverses thousands of years of evolutionary thrust. We are going backwards with our civility and our ability to communicate with one another. Consider the Neanderthal life-style in which cavemen hurriedly ate their food for fear of their food being taken away from them. Millenniums of sensational emotional growth are now being digressed into self-righteous "survival" instincts at our tables in less than 50 years. Why aren't we more upset about this? It takes time to prepare a home-cooked meal. It should not be consumed in less than ten minutes. The table should be set and family members should dine at an agreed time.

Additionally, when we don't dine with each other, we omit opportunities to reflect, respect, and respond. If one cannot identify the problem, how can a solution be found?

Identifying the Problem

CONSIDER THESE CHALLENGES and try to think of ways to improve:

- The need for instant gratification and instant solutions
- Instant messaging which encourages the need to always have the last say
- Obsessive, compulsive electronic usage during meal time
- Poor verbal and written communication skills that have become an accepted norm for how we talk to each other and how we treat each other
- Tardiness and time constraints
- Financial constraints because it takes more funding for a quality lifestyle and in many relationships, both individuals work which leaves less time for good manner focus
- Long work hours and long commutes which lessen quality dining time
- Drive through dining
- Throw-down meals with no course order
- The lack of breakfast for a significant start to the day and short lunch breaks
- The swag bag to-go meal interrupting the dining experience
- Dining in stages to accommodate various family members' schedules.
- The false perception that very casual is more "cool" and therefore acceptable
- Consistent behavior patterns of whining while dining
- High volume dining music that inhibits conversation

If an entity existed that would obviously threaten our family bonds, threaten our quality of life as we know it, and expel our core values, we would fight back. Yet, complacently, we invite convenience and self-absorbed electronic transmissions into our table experiences. We relent; we submissively agree to poor manners and poor language skills. We are coached into dividing life into two distinct over-simplified marketing concepts: we like this or we dislike that. By our nature, we care about our own likeability. Likeability testimonials are even admissible into courts of law. Yet, the most offensive table manners are accepted and not shunned. If one wishes to observe a microcosm of dining styles, dine on a cruise ship. There are the elbow imposers, the conversation dominators, and the experts who are not experts. Then, there are the uniformly messy eaters and the predictably hurried eaters. There even exists an unpleasant dining style from those who choose to verbally insult those who are dining together at the table.

The attentive table companion memorizes the names of those at the table and considers some interesting talking points before coming to the table. The meal should flow around good conversation, without the focus placed on any noticeable *faux pas* from outstanding manner dysfunction. Political labels are dangerous, offensive, and fallacious. Reinforce the concept of the language of good table manners by coming to the table to enjoy life. Don't come to the table to judge and to categorize. Come to the table to grow in character and develop one's communication skills.

The most basic consideration of good dining is to not call too much attention to one's self. One's personal dining space should be respected and kept as neat as possible. Grandmothers have been correct. It is important to sit up straight and to never talk with one's mouth full of food. One should hydrate frequently in order to digest one's food. Beverages with stemware should be held by the stem and not with one's hand covering the bowl part of the glass. This is because the warmth from one's hand will raise the temperature of the liquid in the bowl of the glass.

How Do We Show Dining Respect?

- By genuinely caring for and enjoying the company of those at the table
- By turning off electronic devices
- By assisting an elderly person or others with their chairs
- By utilizing one's napkin, upon arrival at the table
- By being attentive and good conversationalists
- By drawing others into discussions
- By waiting until all dining companions' food is served, per course, before eating
- By participating with good manners
- By passing food items counterclockwise
- By using the correct utensils while eating:

If one is still enjoying the meal and just taking a dining break, the fork and knife are positioned in a "^" shape, pointed to top of the plate.

- By properly cutting the food selection, a piece at a time, instead of cutting up the entire food selection upon the food being served
- By positioning the utensils correctly at the closure of each course:

Spoons go onto the saucer and the backside of the bowl or the cup
Forks and knives, upon course completion, go in a 6:00 position, together, on the plate

- By correctly drinking from water goblets, stemware, teacups, and/or coffee cups

- By excusing one's self from the table, if an exit is needed
- By only putting one's napkin back onto the table at the completion of the meal, to the left of the plate
- By thanking the chef, host, hostess, or parent

Things That Strengthen Dining Skills and Encourage Good Table Manners

- Setting the table (even the night before)
- Being on time for meals
- Taking a deep breath to actually inhale the aromas of the food, prior to eating
- Having respect for one's nourishment – many say a blessing
- Focusing on the conscience act of listening and not interrupting
- Having an interesting table discussion: sustenance with substance
- Planning participatory and enjoyable dining at least one time per week
- Creating thoughtfully planned meals with at least two to three courses
- Developing one's entertainment style for the joy of the dining experience
- Frequently saying please and thank you

MANY ARE UNABLE to eat at a properly set table during lunchtime because of a short lunch break or because of the need to complete their work. Try to compensate for lost quality table time by prioritizing the home dining experience. At the very least, once per week, set a goal to have a quality dining experience demonstrating respect. In our recent history, retail stores were closed on Sundays and many people participated in a

"Sunday" family dinner. Now, with Sunday shopping convenience, with family members living in different cities, and with the need for extra sleep because of long work hours, the dining concept has eroded. Let's call attention to the need to preserve the vital moments created by dining. It is necessary to carve out the time. Preserve and protect it. Emphasize quality not quantity. If cooking is not the choice; then, utilize a restaurant or a private club that reinforces meaningful table traditions. Lead and be consistent. Implement a strategy to guard against complacency. The dining experience needs be *"joie de vivre"* – the joy of living.

The Language of Good Table Manners Through Character Development

Civility: Civility is not based on pretenses and arrogance. It is based on common sense and consideration for others.

Honesty: Yes, honesty is defined through our civil laws; but, it is important to be honest with one's self.

Conversation: There are some people who yell when they talk. Generally speaking, two yellers tend to converse that way in order to be heard. Many times the person who speaks the least, but who speaks with wisdom will be heard the most. Great conversations are enhanced through the dining experiences at our tables. Good listening skills are equally important, as a form of good communication.

Charity: When we think of others and do things for others, we are not thinking of ourselves. Charity benefits the greater good and also charity, to people in need, builds one's self-esteem by taking positive action. Caring and sharing is reinforced at the table.

Ethnic Respect: Let's go beyond political correctness. The judgment calls based on discrimination generate fear and anger. It is simply called respect, period. Communicate person to person through the language of good table manners.

International Relations: Due to technological advances which allow us to travel about the world in one day and due to advanced international communications, international trade has never been more vital. Consider learning the customs of other world regions without assuming that one's own standards apply. Apply flexibility and sensitivity.

Respect for Our Teachers: In the last fifty years, there have been two significant paradigm changes with those who teach us. One is the extreme criticism of those who teach in classrooms. The second is the pack mentally which pushes an agenda that it is not socially acceptable to like to learn. This puts teachers in the position of not being respected. It is time to implement good attitudes, which are generated from positive dining practices.

Hospitality Confidence: Our tables are the basis for how we learn, how we respect each other, and how we transition into the future. Hospitality confidence reinforces kitchen and dining confidence.

Stabilizing Change: Change occurs constantly and recognizing the impacts from change are vital in order to stabilize respectable dining.

Creativity and Learning: Learn to plan ahead. Research and try new recipes. Take cooking classes to improve dining moments.

Embrace the Moment: The dining experience should allow one to feel as though they are exactly where they should be at that exact moment in time.

Overly Casual Is Not Progressive: Respect one's self by practicing good hygiene and by wearing clean attire.

Learning the Language of Good Table Manners

In order to accelerate the understanding of the language of good table manners, it is essential to embrace the protocol for dining etiquette. One can design a table experience with just one course of food to multiple courses. The following descriptions are for eleven dining stages, in course order. These eleven phases provide an overview, which will open the door to learning the new language of good table manners. As the menu designer, decide which courses will be served, but keep the consecutive structure, listed, for a fine dining style.

International culinary beverage suggestions are included, below, although many may choose to refrain from alcoholic beverages. With consideration to those with religious preferences, with age restrictions, and/or with personal choices, the following are only suggestions based on popular beverages for fine dining. If a participant does not or should not drink alcohol, then serve natural spring water or sparkling natural mineral water.

If a participant has allergies, health needs, or does not eat certain foods for religious reasons; then, it is the responsibility of that person to let the cook, the host, or the hostess know in advance. If the guest neglects to notify the person preparing the food in advance, the responsibility falls upon the cook, the host, or the hostess to adapt to those specific needs.

Regarding silverware, each utensil is styled for functionality. As a reminder, as each course is served, it is important to remember that all participants need to wait until all have been served that course at the table before taking a bite of food from one's plate.

Course Order for Quality Dining

1) **Hors d'oeuvres** can be served with *aperitifs (cocktails)*, sparkling wine, and/or Champagne. An example would be to serve bite size canapés, passed upon arrival. It is acceptable to eat with one's fingers.

2) **The Appetizer Course** (sometimes called the "Starter" Course) is traditionally served at the table with a white wine. An example would be a shrimp cocktail or raw oysters, with the appropriate utensil such as a seafood cocktail fork or an oyster fork. Escargots are served with escargot tongs and escargot forks. The seafood cocktail fork, upon course completion, is set on the backside of the saucer, when a shrimp cocktail is served. The base plate (charger plate) is utilized at the place setting and stays in place; but, the saucer holding the appetizer is removed upon completion of the course.

3) **The Soup Course** is served at the table, traditionally, with a white wine or a Sherry. (Sherry is a suggested pairing if Sherry has been an added ingredient to the soup recipe selection.) There are three basic styles of soup spoons: bouillon (hot broth); cream (hot soup made with milk or cream); and gumbo (hot chunky ingredients). There are four basic styles of soup bowls: coupe (a simple, shallow bowl); cream (a two-handled bowl); rimmed (a bowl with a ledge); and footed (a bowl with a pedestal base). A saucer should be under each bowl, when served. Fresh melons, such as honeydew, can be hulled-out to provide soup vessels and, also, a round loaf of bread, hulled-out, can serve as a bowl. Chilled soup can be served in a coupe bowl. When eating, the appropriate spoon is inserted into the soup and then pulled to the back edge of the vessel to clear away any drips. Then, the soup is ingested. This stroke, towards the back rim of the bowl,

is to occur with each spoonful. One does not blow on the soup to cool it. It can be cooled by gently stirring, without clicking the utensil against the bowl. Unless it is Oriental soup, which is served with a ceramic spoon, one does not adjust the bowl or tilt the bowl to accommodate the last spoonful. Upon completion of the soup course, the spoon is placed on the backside of the saucer. Please note that the base plate (charger plate) is still utilized at the place setting.

4) **The Fish Course** is served at the table, traditionally, with a white wine. This is served prior to the main course; so, the portion should be small. The utensils recommended are a fish fork and a fish knife. The designs of the utensils vary from the manufacturers and the designs have changed through the centuries. A well-made fish knife will be perfectly balanced between the blade and the handle, which adds dexterity with the removal of any fish bones. Generally, the blade has a hook curve. The coordinating fish fork may or may not have a hook curve in one of the prongs to assist with the removal of any fish bones. The base plate (charger plate) is still utilized at the place setting. One should cut a small piece of the fish, a piece at a time, and not cut up the entire fish dish, upon being served. The fork and the knife, set at rest position, are positioned in a "^" shape, pointing up. The fork and the knife, upon course completion, are set at a 6:00 position, together on the plate.

5) **The Sorbet** selection is served to cleanse the palate, following the fish course. It is not necessary to serve sorbet if a seafood selection is not served; however, it is permissible. The sorbet spoon is smaller than a teaspoon and the sorbet cup should be served on a saucer. Upon completion of the course, the spoon is to be set on the backside of the saucer. The base plate (charger plate) is still utilized at the place setting; however, the base plate should be removed when the sorbet is removed because the main course plate is not to be set on top of the base plate.

6) **The Main Course** is the entrée and a significant focus. It is traditionally served with a red and/or a white wine. Selections vary from beef, veal, poultry, lamb, pork, seafood, and/or vegetarian. There can be a combination of two proteins on the same plate, paired with a vegetable and a

starch. It is advised to be sensitive to any dietary needs and/or religious requirements in order to not compromise or offend any dining participants. Again, if a guest has dietary needs and/or religious requirements, it is the responsibility of the guest to let the host or hostess know in advance. This knowledge will provide a cohesive dining moment. If that is overlooked, then the responsibility falls upon the host or hostess to provide the appropriate plating. Poor communication could cause a great delay in service. The utensils are a place (dinner) fork and a place (dinner) knife. If a steak is served, then a steak knife should be provided. One should cut one piece of the entrée, at a time, and not cut up the entire food selection, upon being served. The fork and the knife, set at rest position, are positioned in a "∧" shape, pointing up. The fork and the knife, set upon course completion, are set at a 6:00 position, together on the plate.

7) **The Salad Course** can be served prior to the entrée or after the entrée. Please note that many countries in North America and South America tend to serve the salad before the main course. Many European countries offer the salad course after the main course. These are personal choices. White wine can be served with the salad course. The salad course can consist of all greens or with a mixture of fruit. Whether the salad is served before or after the main course, the salad portion should be small because of the multiple courses. The utensils are a salad fork and a salad knife, which should be near the same length. It is recommended to have the salad ingredients pre-cut so that a minimum amount of cutting is needed at the table. The fork and the knife, set at rest position, are positioned in a "∧" shape, pointing up. The fork and the knife, set upon course completion, are set at a 6:00 position, together on the plate.

8) **The Cheese Course** is very versatile. It is recommended to serve the cheese course with a port wine, a red wine, or a white wine. Many times this course substitutes for the dessert course. It may be served with interesting bread, nuts, and fruit. It is appropriate to offer more than one cheese selection. Examples of blue cheeses are: Danablu (from Denmark); Gorgonzola PDO (from Lombardia and Piedmont in Italy); Roquefort AOC (from the Mid-Pyrénées region of France); and Stilton PDO (from

Britain). When serving a good blue cheese, honey is an appropriate accompaniment. Other cheese examples are: Emmentaler (from Switzerland); Jarlsberg (from Norway); Port Salut (from France); and Wensleydale (from Britain). It is suggested to serve this course with a small cheese fork and a cheese knife. Different manufacturers make different styles. The cheese fork and the cheese knife should be about the same the length. The fork and the knife, set at rest position, are positioned in a "^" shape, pointing up. The fork and the knife, upon course completion, are set at a 6:00 position, together on the plate.

9) **The Dessert Course,** traditionally, is the grand finale. Champagne or sparkling wine is the traditional beverage of choice; although, coffee and tea are completely acceptable. The dessert choices range from hot to cold and flambéed to artfully designed. It is a good idea to have desserts available that are sugar-free when entertaining multiple guests.

This is the significant celebration recognition course. Toasts to the celebrants (with alcoholic or non-alcoholic beverages) are recommended during the dessert course. It is not good etiquette to clang on the glass with a utensil to gain the attention of others. It is the honor of host or hostess to give the first toast. When toasting, the person giving the toast should stand up and hold the glass, by the stem, in his left hand, nearest his heart, which is the modern consideration. Protocol purists will insist that the glass should be held in the right hand. This is a personal choice. The person giving the toast should address those gathered with a projected tone to gain the attention of the guests. Those receiving the toast should hold their glasses, by the stems, in their right hands, while staying seated. It is acceptable to tip the glasses together, with those near. If there is a designated person conducting a special toast, it is considerate to let that person know of his or her role in advance. That person may want to prepare thoughtful words for the occasion. Also, the designated person may drink less alcoholic beverage until the task is completed, if that person knows in advance.

It is recommended to serve this course with a dessert fork (for cake), an ice cream fork (for ice cream), and/or a dessert spoon (for puddings or soufflés). The dessert spoon and the dessert fork should be about the same length. An ice cream fork has a short handle, by design. Upon completion of the course, the dessert utensils are set at a 6:00 position, together on the dessert plate. If a bowl and saucer are used, then, the ice cream fork, and/or dessert spoon should be set on the backside of the saucer. It is rare that all three utensils will be needed for one dessert presentation.

10) **The Demitasse (Coffee) Course** is served with bite size chocolates called petits fours. A demitasse spoon should be utilized with espresso coffee which is served in a demitasse cup and set onto a saucer. Coffee cups and saucers should be utilized when serving basic coffee. This course encourages conversation. The spoon is set onto the backside of the saucer, after usage.

11) **After Dinner Beverages**, also known as *digestifs*, are frequently offered in a separate room for socialization and for long, lingering conversation. These can include brandy, limoncello, amaretto, or liqueurs. Hot tea or coffee should be offered, also.

These courses, during one evening, represent the complete indulgence in dining dynamics. A single course of soup is an honorable meal and should be treated with respect. A meaningful dining experience can be enjoyed with one or two courses. The concept described above is the course order for formal dining; but, please recall that the food selections consist of small portions. Strive for quality dining, not quantity dining. Historically, dining etiquette has been based on logic and the utensils are based on functionality.

Being A Connoisseur Is Not Necessary

WHEN WINE IS poured, a commentary is customary. Formally, wine is sampled by the host or the hostess and then it is poured for the guests. It is considered good manners to fill the ladies' glasses first, beginning with the most prominent guest. Wine pouring service is not poured counterclockwise, as with items passed around the table amongst the guests. The person pouring the wine should pour clockwise because it allows the server to walk forward as he or she pours instead of walking backwards. Also, the label of the bottle needs to face out so that guests can see what is being poured. The experienced pourer should not use a napkin under the bottle neck to prevent spills. This takes skill and practice.

With commentary expected, some may be inclined to speak about the wine without knowing the subject matter. This frequently occurs when a guest wants to be included in the conversation; however, a lack of knowledge about any subject could prove to be embarrassing for a person expounding or irritating to the other guests. If one has not marginally researched wine selections, then it is best to refrain from the wine commentary. It is very easy to learn about wine in order to be included in the wine commentary. The following three concepts are frequently misunderstood.

As a simplification, Bordeaux wines are definitely from the region in France known as Bordeaux. Many fine and famous Cabernet Sauvignon wines are produced in Bordeaux. In recent history, other regions of the world have begun to produce fine Cabernet Sauvignon wines; however, those cannot be called Bordeaux wines because the wines are not produced in Bordeaux, France. We simply call those wines Cabernet Sauvignon selections. So, when one looks at a daunting multi-page wine list and sees a page of red Bordeaux wines and a page of Cabernet Sauvignon wines, both references were produced using the same grape variety, Cabernet Sauvignon. Let's take it a step further. The region of Bordeaux has a large land area. Many white wines are produced in Bordeaux. These white wines are not produced from Cabernet Sauvignon grapes. The white wines from this region are known as white Bordeaux wines. Another indication of a Bordeaux wine selection is to look at the shape of the short neck bottle (with high "shoulders").

Likewise, as an explanation, Burgundy wines are definitely from the region in France known as Burgundy. Many fine and famous Pinot noir wines are produced in Burgundy. In recent history, other regions of the world have begun to produce fine Pinot noir wines; however, those cannot be called Burgundy wines because the wines are not produced in Burgundy, France. We simply call those wines Pinot noir selections. So, when one looks at that multi-page wine list and sees a page of red Burgundy wines and a page of Pinot noir wines, both references were produced with the same grape variety, Pinot noir. Again, let's take it a step further. The region of Burgundy has a large land area. Many white wines are produced in Burgundy. These white wines are not produced from Pinot noir grapes. The white wines from this region are known as white Burgundy wines. Another indication of a Burgundy wine selection is to look at the shape of the long neck bottle (with rounded "shoulders").

Additionally, many are confused about the difference between Champagne and sparkling wine. Geographically, Champagne produced in the French region of Champagne is called Champagne. By contrast, sparkling wine is produced in other regions of the world; however, some producers of champagne in California label their bottles as California Champagne. Rosé Champagne or pink sparkling wine are optional champagne blends. The focus is that both Champagnes and sparkling wines are bubbly, celebratory beverages. The labeling is based on the laws that govern the products' disclosure in that specific region.

It takes years of wine study to become an expert. A casual conversation about wine is encouraged; but, the advice is to think before speaking. Expertise without being an authentic expert creates inaccuracies and impacts the dining experience. By tasting wines, one will discover favorites. Pairing wine with food has some general guidelines such as white wine with fish and red wine with beef; but, the best pairing is done by pre-tasting the food selection with a wine consideration, prior to an occasion.

Wine selections are vast and it is entertaining to explore the wonderful choices. In Bordeaux, it is a tradition to drink the oldest wine last during dinner. Customs and traditions may create a break in international protocol standards. An example would be the custom of *Chabròl*, which is performed in some rural areas in France. It is worth noting because the purpose is to never be wasteful. When the last little bit of soup is left in one's bowl, the last sip of wine is poured into the remaining soup. The individual then uses his or her hands to pick up the bowl and drink the last bit of wine infused soup. To a non-regional visitor, the custom could seem crude; however, when one realizes that starvation was an imposing factor during WWI and WWII, the motive is based on practicality.

Regarding good beverage manners, is advisable to refrain from spilling any of one's wine onto the tablecloth. When one begins to feel the effect of the alcohol, one should refrain from over-indulging. The most important aspect of dining with alcoholic beverage service is that there is a designated driver or that transportation home is prearranged. It is the responsibility of the host and/or hostess to not allow their guest(s) to drive while intoxicated. Additionally, in many countries, it is against the law to serve alcohol to teenagers. Check the drinking age requirements prior to serving alcohol. Another tip is for the host and/or hostess to minimize alcoholic consumption until the end of the meal to ensure that all of the guests' needs are met. A host and/or hostess can enjoy natural spring water or sparkling natural mineral water for hydration.

So Simple, So Considerate

It is important to be on time. This is especially true for an afternoon tea, since the table duration time is less than that for a dinner.

It is a courtesy to not set one's utensils into the closure position until those dining reach closure with that course. The reason is that some people are very slow eaters. The service staff, host, or hostess should not remove the plates until everyone has completed that course. If the dining participants rush the closure by signaling with their utensils, plates could be removed too early and one or more guests could be rushed.

Napkins should be centered (or placed on the left) at the beginning of the meal. Immediately upon arrival, napkins are to utilized by the table guests. When excusing oneself from the table, the napkin goes onto the seat of the chair. It does not go back on the table until the end of the meal. The attentive server will fold it in half and place it on the back or right arm of the chair. If one wears lipstick, it is considered poor manners to blot one's lipstick onto a lovely napkin. At the completion of the meal, the napkin is gently folded and placed on the left side of the place setting. This can be remembered by placing it on the left side, as a thank you from the heart.

When passing bread counterclockwise, the person picking up the bread plate does not take a piece of bread first. That would be like giving someone a bouquet of flowers and deciding to take a stem for oneself prior to handing the bouquet to the recipient.

Please remember that no purses are to be set on the table and neither are elbows...

In recent history, the respectful tone, of yes, ma'am; no, ma'am; yes, sir; and no, sir, has been discouraged due to connotations of implied supremacy. The proper, respectable substitute is to utilize yes, please or no, thank you. If children are not taught to respect elders, their concepts of respect will develop slower and assimilation of respectful concepts will be more challenging.

"Musical Chairs" The Changing Tempo

For centuries, we have valued our matriarchal and patriarchal seating, with the "heads" of the family positioned at the ends of the table. Today, during many corporate meetings, the top managers are seated in the middle section of the table, with no one seated at the head of the table. This demonstrates a willingness to build team skills and to meet others in the middle. During state dinners, the head of state is seated in the center section of the table arrangement and not at the head of the table. Can innovative seating styles work in our homes? Flexibility is good. Many of our homes are designed for round tables and seating may be limited. These are personal choices.

Formally and traditionally, the female was to be seated to the right of the male. Relationship dynamics have changed. Singles, as well as couples and partners, enjoy dining moments; so, the formal concept is too rigid. Someone may bring a date or a friend who is unfamiliar with those who are gathered. It is the responsibility of the host and/or hostess to learn the guests' names prior to their arrival. If the newcomer is not engaging in conversation, then, the host or hostess should make every effort to include the newcomer in the conversation. There exists a consideration to mix up the "couples" at the table. This is not recommended because it may cause discomfort with a guest who is shy. The point is that seating arrangements are changing and awareness is important.

Gifts for the Dining Experience

IT IS ENCOURAGED for the guests to bring a host or hostess gift upon arrival. A bottle of fine wine and fresh flowers are appropriate. The host or hostess may want to set out table favors, which are fitting; but, these should be small. Caviar spoons tied with bows are excellent favors. The most special gift, to any guest at the table, is to be called by name and to be included in the conversation. Parting gifts, given by the host and/or hostess, are a special gesture demonstrating good manners. Parting gifts could be as simple as copies of the evening's menus tied with ribbons. Also, small baskets of homemade bread bring smiles to guests as they depart. The parting gift gesture gives the host and/or hostess an opportunity for closure with guests who may want to linger too long. All of the guests should thank the host and/or hostess when exiting and then thoughtfully send a written thank you note.

Protocol Correctness (Good Manners) vs. Political Correctness (Artificial Good Manners)

THROUGHOUT THIS BOOK, table conversation is encouraged. It is from this place of strength that we can become table messengers; however, this role comes with responsibilities. Utilize the language of good table manners as the stabilizer. Mistakenly, good manners have recently been confused with political correctness – now a common household term. The correct term is protocol correctness, which sets the standards for courteous behavior. Protocol correctness is not polarizing and it does not encourage judgmental labels that impose on any sensitivities. Protocol correctness is the natural inclination of treating each other well because good manners are innate and easy. Protocol correctness has successfully existed long before political correctness.

In the last few decades, political correctness has been falsely substituted for good verbal communication manners. Political correctness emphasizes the need to be nice in order to not ignite the fury of guests' sensitivities. These artificial good manners have been generated because we have distanced ourselves from our dining table stability – our *true north*. If we focus on politeness, hundreds of years of evolved etiquette standards, and a willingness to emotionally evolve, we do not have to second guess our responses to our guests' needs. The only reason that there is a shift to the superficial, political niceties is because solid, genuine, good manners are being rejected.

If we practice the language of good table manners, political correctness will become a non-issue. If we practice good manners at our tables, we will focus on politeness and considerate behavior. It is all about respect, period.

The Gift of the Functioning Table

EACH GENERATION STRUGGLES with transitions from the past to the future. The dining experience is becoming a lost art. For hundreds of years, silversmiths created wonderful silverware designs for multiple, specific uses. These designs were expected because of the dedicated desire to take great care with dining. Today, plastic utensils are not just for picnics; plastic utensils are frequently used for convenience in our homes. This over-casual dining style has encroached into our language skills, too. The language of good table manners does not encourage a hectic lifestyle, which reinforces interrupted meals. If we consciously combat time constraints and dining negativity, we can prioritize a positive dining experience. Less than a century ago, most had an agrarian, rural lifestyle. Now, we are mostly urbanites. Less than a century ago, farm food went straight to many dining tables, as a one-step process. The rhythm has been interrupted by intense domestic neglect. Less than a century ago, political correctness was not a recognizable term. Take down barriers created by pretentious, poor communication skills and bridge weaknesses with a wholesome, welcoming table that embraces the language of good table manners. We, as a society, are bright and we are able to solve problems. We have the tools; the tools are our silverware. This is our revelry; this is our call to personal civility. Have a seat; it is a place of honor. Generation to generation we will continue to soar by accepting the gifts of our well-deserved places at our own tables through our domestic intellect.

Humbly set this table
Keeping its silver straight
May its bounty be ample
Never to be ungrateful
Surround us with meaningful exchange
Breaking bread of home-grown grains

Risen from once sown fields
May our conversation be the harvest yield.

© Kelly McBride Loft

One should always thank those who are special and who are our lifelong dining companions.
Thank you Michael, Honni, and Nick.

Fish Fork

Place (Entree) Fork

Salad Fork

Cheese Fork

Butter Knife

Dessert Fork

Dessert Spoon

Cheese Knife

Salad Knife

Place Knife

Sorbet Spoon

Fish Knife

Soup Spoon

Seafood Cocktail Fork

(1) A Formal Place Setting of Utensils

(2) A Full Formal Place Setting with Appropriate Glassware

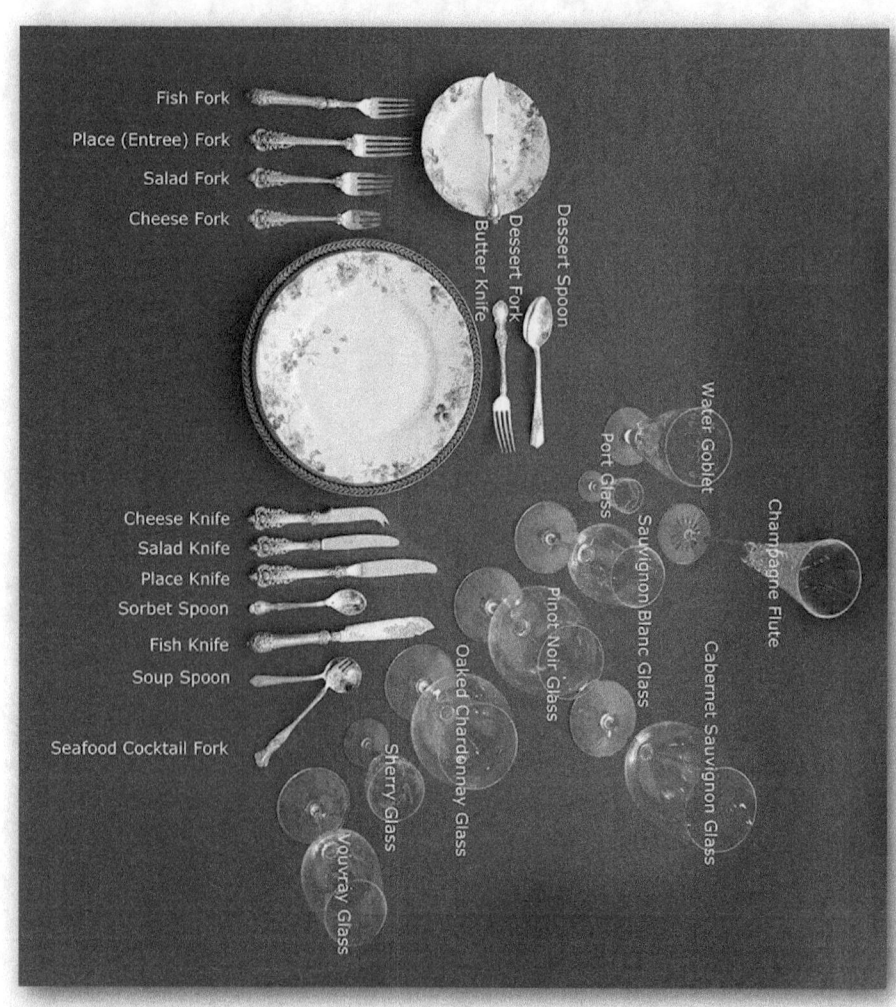

Fish Fork
Place (Entree) Fork
Salad Fork
Cheese Fork

Butter Knife
Dessert Fork
Dessert Spoon

Cheese Knife
Salad Knife
Place Knife
Sorbet Spoon
Fish Knife
Soup Spoon

Seafood Cocktail Fork

Water Goblet
Port Glass
Sauvignon Blanc Glass
Champagne Flute
Pinot Noir Glass
Cabernet Sauvignon Glass
Oaked Chardonnay Glass
Sherry Glass
Vouvray Glass

(3) A Formal Place Setting with Labeled Utensils and Glassware

36

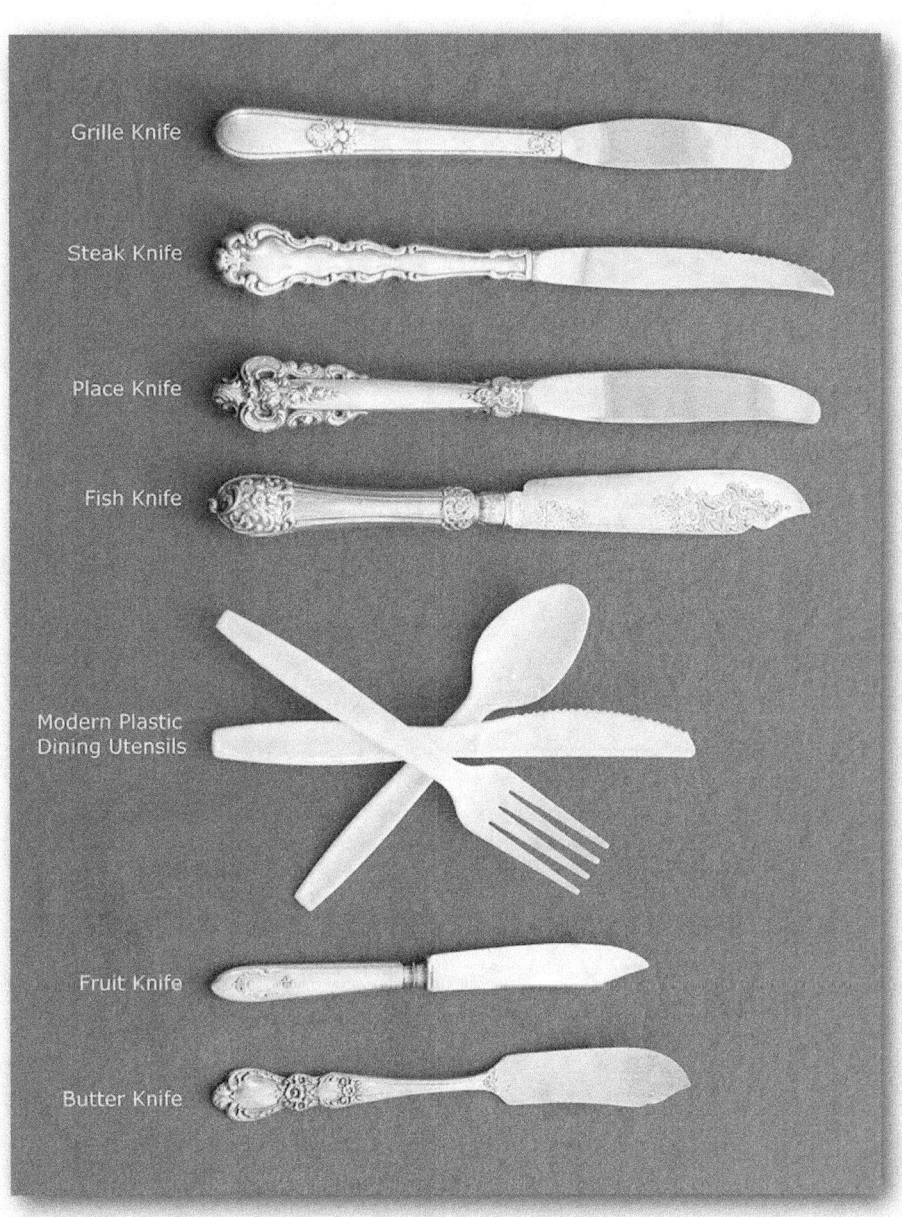

Grille Knife

Steak Knife

Place Knife

Fish Knife

Modern Plastic
Dining Utensils

Fruit Knife

Butter Knife

(4) Knives Based on Functionality

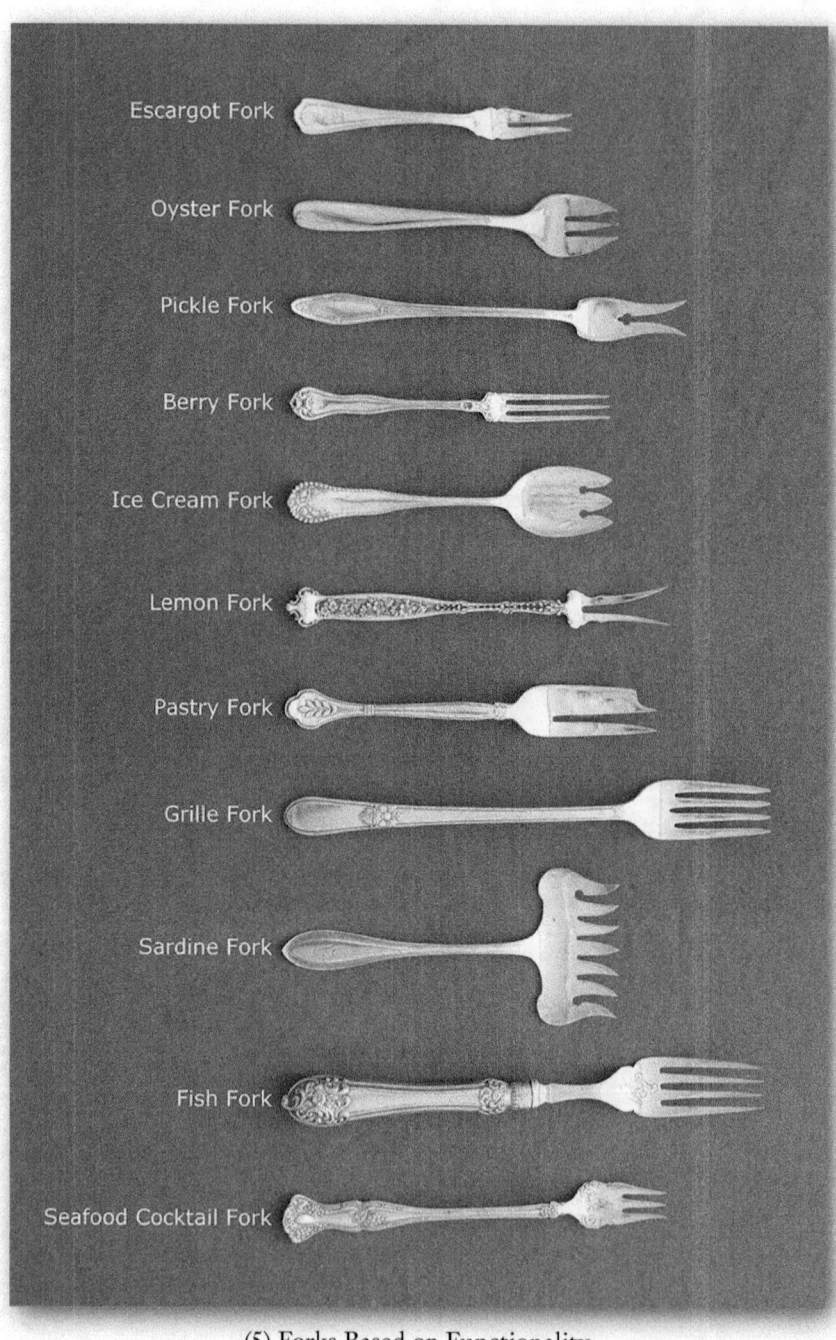

Escargot Fork

Oyster Fork

Pickle Fork

Berry Fork

Ice Cream Fork

Lemon Fork

Pastry Fork

Grille Fork

Sardine Fork

Fish Fork

Seafood Cocktail Fork

(5) Forks Based on Functionality

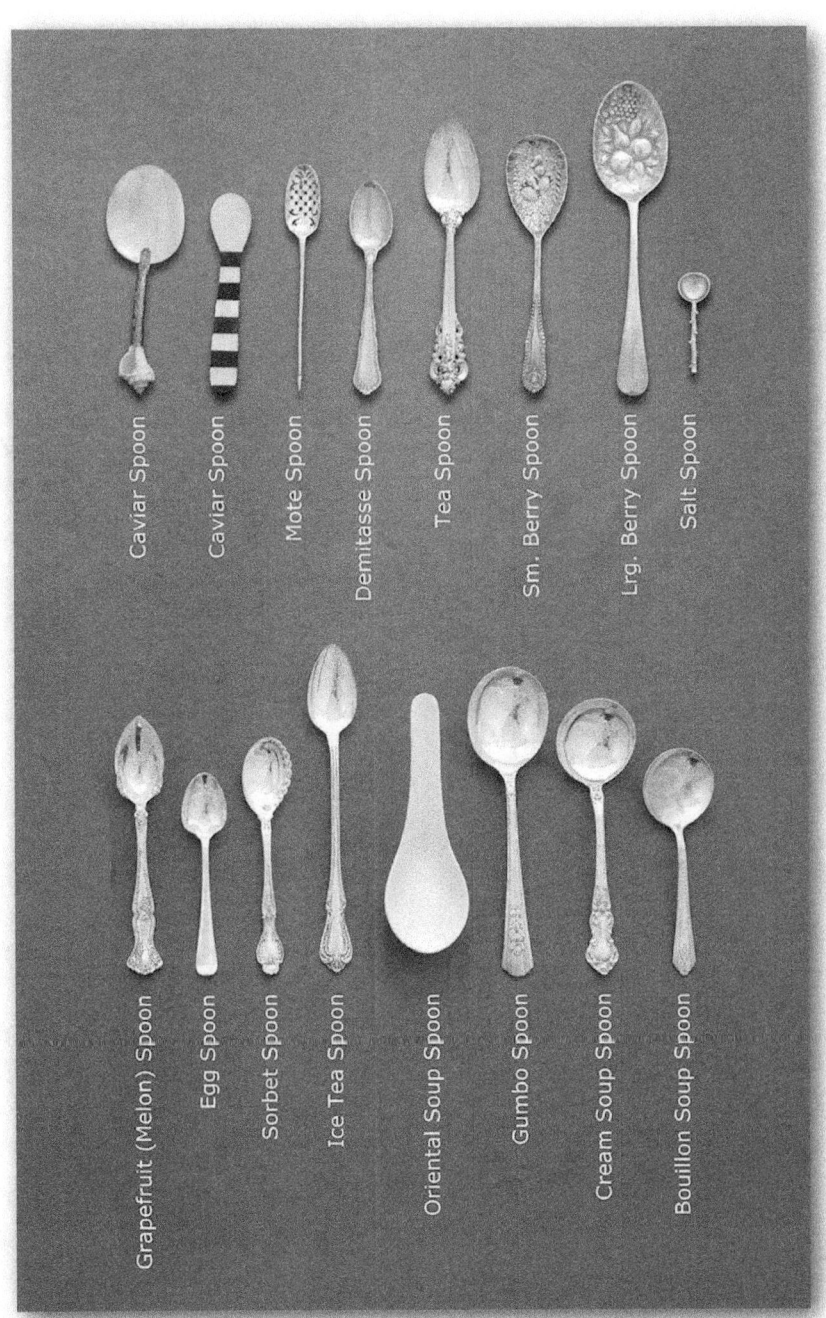

(6) Spoons Based on Functionality

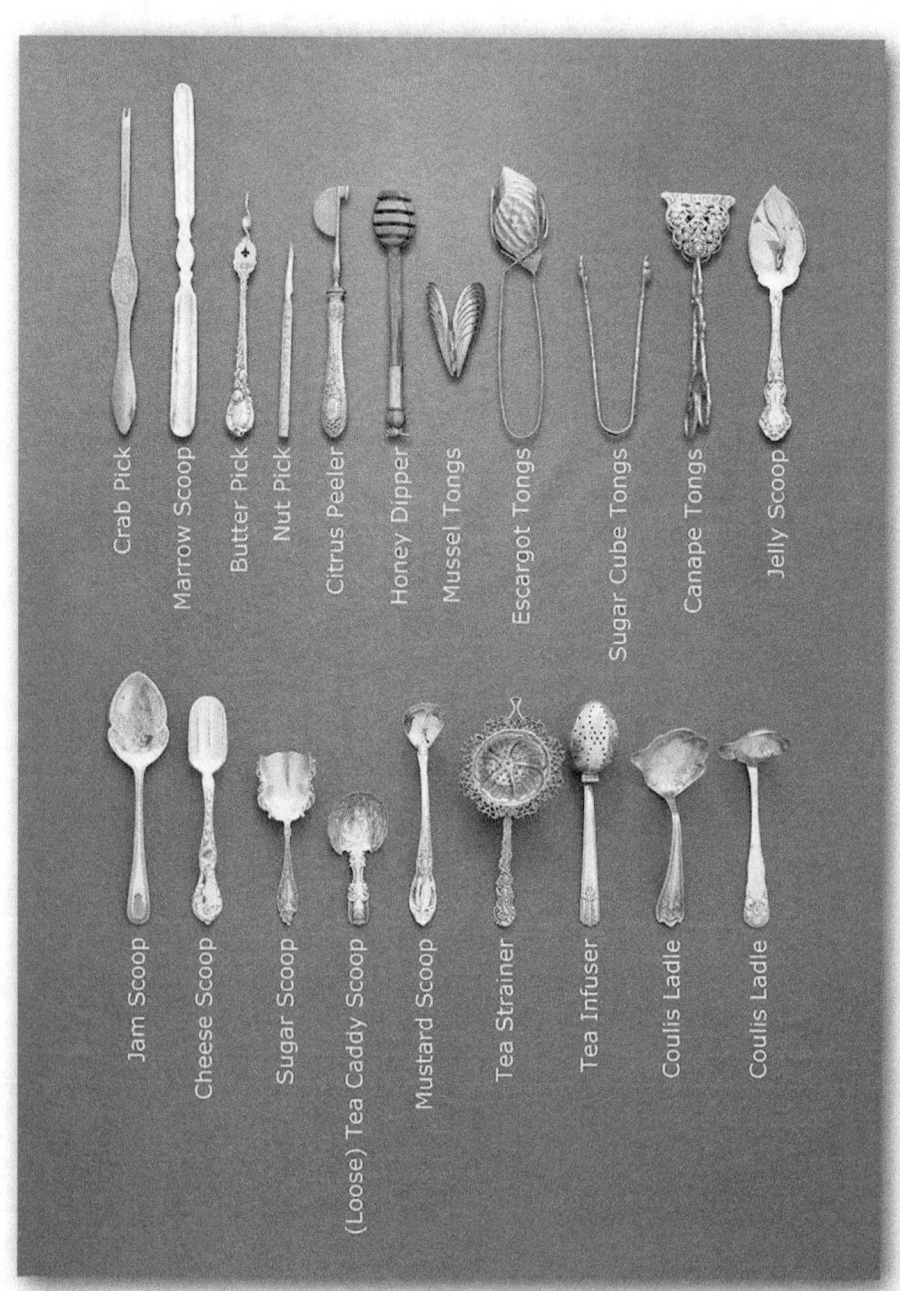

Crab Pick

Marrow Scoop

Butter Pick

Nut Pick

Citrus Peeler

Honey Dipper

Mussel Tongs

Escargot Tongs

Sugar Cube Tongs

Canape Tongs

Jelly Scoop

Jam Scoop

Cheese Scoop

Sugar Scoop

(Loose) Tea Caddy Scoop

Mustard Scoop

Tea Strainer

Tea Infuser

Coulis Ladle

Coulis Ladle

(7) Special Utensils Based on Functionality

(8) Beverage Vessels

41

Cream Soup Bowl

Footed Soup Bowl

Coupe (Bouillon) Bowl

Whimsical Soup Bowl

Rimmed Soup Bowl

(9) Bowl Designs

About the Author

KELLY MCBRIDE LOFT, a culinary artist, shares her repertoire of skillful dining knowledge and trusted entertaining techniques. It is from her international canvas that she paints, with words, the illumination of teachable table opportunities. Kelly has designed events for President George H. W. Bush, ambassadors, and international dignitaries. She has decades of experience as an event designer, with formal culinary training in Europe. Kelly has lived and studied in Europe with advanced studies at the Cordon Bleu Cookery School, London; pastry certification from LaVarenne Culinary School in Burgundy, France; and The Art of French Pastry studies at the Ritz Escoffier Culinary School in Paris. She teaches dining etiquette to adults and children; event planning; international tea exploration; tea etiquette; and the art of the silver tea service. Kelly has authored over 27 books creating the Plan Like A Chef™ book series which focuses on dining etiquette, event planning, and celebration development. She continues to showcase her skills as a professional pastry chef, as an event designer, as an internationally acclaimed author, and as a food writer. Kelly also produces a weekly culinary blog with recipes and entertaining advice titled "Celebration Logic" which can be found her website *www.eventplanningbooks.net*. From fine dining to contemporary culinary simplicity, Kelly's emphasis is on *"joie de vivre"* – the joy of living, so that others may embrace joyful table moments.